70035
CBS
ORIGINAL LONDON CAST ALBUM
DELFONT
FIELDING
I. MICHAELS
present

Juliet Prowse

Sweet Charity

Book
NEIL SIMON
Music
CY COLEMAN
Lyrics
DOROTHY FIELDS
Based on original screenplay by
FEDERICO FELLINI
Scenery and Lighting
ROBERT RANDOLPH
Costumes
IRENE SHARAFF
Orchestrations
RALPH BURNS
Original Production staged and choreographed by
BOB FOSSE
London Production Directed by
LAWRENCE CARR
Musical numbers and dances staged by
ED GASPER
Musical Direction
ALYN AINSWORTH
Musical Associate
RAY COOK
ORIGINAL NEW YORK PRODUCTION
by FRYER, CARR AND HARRIS

Juliet Prowse in the 1967 West End cast recording.

Sweet Charity
DEBBIE ALLEN as SWEET CHARITY
BROADWAY CAST ALBUM
A Digital Recording

Debbie Allen in the 1986 Broadway cast recording.

Christina Applegate in the 2005 Broadway cast recording.

Molly Ringwald is the "bravest individual" in the 2006 touring production.

Sweet Charity

Sweet Charity (b.1966) is just entering the prime of life, heralded by a dazzling New York run in 2005 and followed by a national tour. Christina Applegate has already taken her place among the memorable stars who have coveted and set ablaze the title role: Debbie Allen, Shirley MacLaine, Juliet Prowse, and the founding Charity, Gwen Verdon.

The choreography still expresses the fierce, witty energy of its creator, Bob Fosse (who also conceived and staged the original production), via four crackling, large ensemble pieces: "Big Spender," "Rich Man's Frug," "Rhythm of Life," and "I'm a Brass Band."

That Neil Simon returned to the show to lovingly touch up the book for its revival is testament to the grip still exerted on that creative giant by the timeless story of "a girl who wanted to be loved." The archetypal New York scene—two strangers stuck in an elevator—is his great tour de force in *Sweet Charity*, but his one-liners are right up there:

Rookie dance hall hostess: "I don't dance very well."

Veteran hostess: "Who dances? We defend ourselves to music."

This face-to-face between naiveté and hard-won experience is a major theme of the story, and in the warmly-human Ms. Charity Hope Valentine, ambivalence bubbles along hilariously and poignantly.

In the opening scene, Charity receives *not* the expected proposal of marriage from her "boyfriend," but a push into the Central Park lake. And, he steals her purse! So Charity arrives a little late to her job as dance hall hostess at the Fandango Ballroom. She knows her girlfriend is right in admonishing, "You run your heart like a hotel—you got guys checking in and out all the time!" But the knowledge never short-circuits her capacity for connecting to a fellow human. When she has a late-night visit to the pad of an Italian movie star of a certain age (nothing happens!), the scene is full of big laughs but, wonderfully, a strange rapport develops between them that we really want to believe in.

Last to arrive on the scene, through yet another chance encounter (in the aforementioned stalled elevator) is Oscar, needy and creepy, but inspired—possibly by Charity's warmth and energy—to the very brink of commitment. After a loving send-off by her pals at the Fandango, the couple heads off to be married.... But the plot belongs to Federico Fellini, and Oscar can't get it done, can't overcome his neurotic immaturity. Charity is devastated and lets us (and him) know it. But her bottom line is "I'm the bravest individual I have ever met...there's always tomorrow."

And the songs! Music by Cy Coleman. Words by my mother, Dorothy Fields. As a professional musician, I've played these songs separately for years, but when I hear one after another in a performance of *Sweet Charity*, I feel the true potency of that score. Cy's writing doesn't grab attention for itself. It's always supportive of the story. Yet, two of his melodies have achieved the status of instantly recognizable standard: "If My Friends Could See Me Now" and "Big Spender." He's special to me—the last real jazz guy to write Broadway scores.

I once asked Cy how he and Dorothy got together. Apparently, after an ASCAP meeting, he suggested they try collaborating. Dorothy's reply was so typical of her: "Well, I've been wondering when you were going to ask!" She had long been among the most celebrated and successful songwriters of the greatest generation of songwriters, but I think she was unique in accomplishing a second go-round with an equally talented partner a generation younger than herself and then producing work equal to her historic best. She made every word count.

It was a dream team that crafted *Sweet Charity* and their work stands a good chance of staying vibrant as long as people go to musicals.

David Lahm
September, 2007

CONTENTS

© Don Hunstein

Goddard Lieberson, producer of the original Broadway cast recording, along with Cy Coleman, musical director Fred Werner, Dorothy Fields, Gwen Verdon, and Bob Fosse.

YOU SHOULD SEE YOURSELF

Music by CY COLEMAN
Lyrics by DOROTHY FIELDS

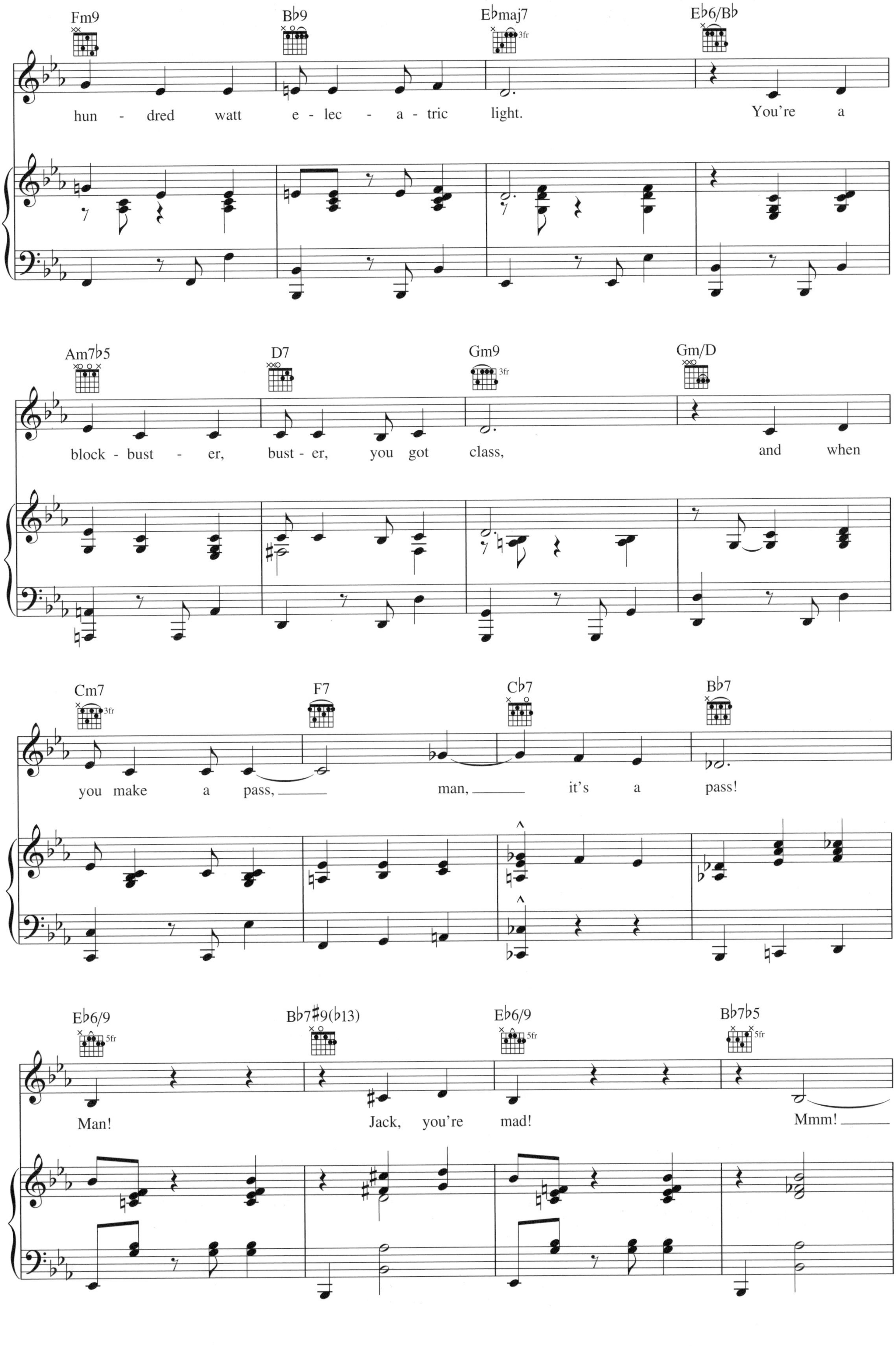
Fm9 B♭9 E♭maj7 E♭6/B♭
3fr
hun - dred watt e - lec - a - tric light. You're a
Am7♭5 D7 Gm9 Gm/D
3fr
block - bust - er, bust - er, you got class, and when
Cm7 F7 C♭7 B♭7
3fr
you make a pass, man, it's a pass!
E♭6/9 B♭7♯9(♭13) E♭6/9 B♭7♭5
5fr 5fr 5fr
Man! Jack, you're mad! Mmm!

E♭6/9
Cm7/B♭
Am7♭5
A♭m7
D♭9
How those corn - y jokes turn me
G♭maj9
G♭6/D♭
Fm9
B♭9
on! And I laugh till I'm ga - ga - ga - ga -
E♭maj7
B♭6
Am7
Gm7
C9
gone! When you switch to a se - duc - a - tive
Fmaj9
F6/C
Fm7
Cm/E♭
mood, I'm not stuck on you, lov - er,

Dm7♭5
F(add2)/C
G7/D
Cm
3fr
I am glued!
In that col - lege type
Gm7
Cm
3fr
rah - rah - dee - dah tweed,
do I wilt?
Gm7
Cm
3fr
Boy, are you built!
You're so strong, you got
Gm7
Cm
3fr
mus - cles you don't need!
Yes,
3

F7♭5
B♭9
E♭6/9
B♭7♯9(♭13)
yes in - deed!
Wild!
Dad, you're
E♭6/9
B♭7♭5
E♭6/9
Cm7/B♭
Am7♭5
wild!
Grrrr.
You should
A♭m7
D♭9
G♭maj9
G♭6/D♭
see your - self in my eyes!
You're a
Fm9
B♭9
Gm7
C7
blue rib - bon Pu - lit - it - zer Prize!
You should

Am7♭5
A♭m7(add13)
E♭(add2)/G
Cm7
Cm7/B♭
see your - self and in -
Am7♭5
A♭m7(add13)
E♭(add2)/G
Cm7
Cm7/B♭
spect your - self. Get a
Am7♭5
A♭m7(add13)
E♭(add2)/G
Cm7
Cm7/B♭
mir - ror, man, and re -
F9
Cm7/F
E♭+/F
Fm9/C
flect your - self. You should

E♭/B♭
6fr
E♭+/B♭
Cm/B♭
8fr
E♭7/B♭
6fr
see your - self as
Fm7/B♭
B♭7(add13)
6fr
I
see you
E♭6
B♭m7/E♭
6fr
E♭6
B♭m7/E♭
6fr
now!
E♭6
B♭m7/E♭
6fr
E♭6

BIG SPENDER

Music by CY COLEMAN
Lyrics by DOROTHY FIELDS

Bb
E7
I don't pop my cork for ev - 'ry guy I see.
Dm
To Coda
N.C.
Bb7
A7
N.&H.:
ALL:
Hey! Big spend - er!
Spend
a lit - tle time with
Dm
N.C.
NICKIE:
me.
Do you like to have
D
Dmaj7
D6
Em
Em(maj7)
Em7
HELENE:
ALL:
fun, fun, fun? How's a - bout a few
laughs, laughs?
I can show you a

B♭9
A9
B♭9
A13
D.S. al Coda
good time. Let me show you a good time. The min-ute you
CODA
N.C.
N.&H.:
E♭m
N.C.
ALL:
Dm
Hey, big spend-er! Hey, big spend-er!
B♭9
A9
Dm
Spend a lit-tle time with me. Spend a lit-tle time with
Dm6/9
me. Spend a lit-tle time with me.

RICH MAN'S FRUG

Music by CY COLEMAN
Lyrics by DOROTHY FIELDS

E♭m
A♭
E♭m
A♭
E♭m
B
Em
Em/D
Em/C♯
Em/C
F♯(add♭9)
B5
F♯(add♭9)
B5
N.C.
Em
A
Em
A
Em
C
Fm
D♭

N.C.
Fm
D♭7
ff
p
ff
Fm
p
D♭7
C7♯5
D♭7
C7♯5
Fm
Em
E♭m
Dm
cresc.
f
D♭m
Cm
Bm
B♭m
Am
A♭m
Gm
C

Fm
B♭
Fm
B♭
Fm
C♯
F♯m
B
F♯m
p
B
F♯m
D
Gm
3fr
cresc. poco a poco
E♭
3fr
N.C.
f
Gm
3fr
C
Gm
3fr
Gm6/9
3fr

IF MY FRIENDS COULD SEE ME NOW

Music by CY COLEMAN
Lyrics by DOROTHY FIELDS

A
D♯7
G♯7
C♯m
I'd like those stum - ble bums to see for a fact
I'd hear those thrift shop cats say: "Broth - er! get her!
I hear my bud - dies say - ing: "Cra - zy! What gives?
F♯7
B7
the kind of top drawer, first - rate chums I at - tract!
Draped on a bed - spread made of three kinds of fur!"
To - night she's liv - ing like the oth - er half lives."
E
Emaj7
E7
All I can say is, "Wow - ee!" Look - a where I am.
All I can say is, "Wow!" Wait till the riff and raff
To think the high - est brow, which I must say is he,
A
Amaj7
G♯7
To - night I land - ed, pow! right in a pot of jam!
see just ex - act - ly how he signed this au - to - graph!
should pick the low - est brow, which there's no doubt is me.

C♯7
F♯7
What a set - up!
What a build up!
What a step up!
Ho - ly cow! They'd nev - er be - lieve it, if my
1, 2
B7
E
friends could see me now!
8va
F♯7
B7
If they could
3
F♯m9
2fr
F♯m6/9
Amaj7/B
friends could see
B7(add13)
E
me now!

TOO MANY TOMORROWS

Music by CY COLEMAN
Lyrics by DOROTHY FIELDS

Am7♭5
D7
Gm
3fr
Gm7/C
C7
Fmaj7
me? Too man - y to - mor - rows I sim - ply can - not face.
F6/9
B♭m9
6fr
E♭7♭9
5fr
A♭maj9
3fr
Those pas - sion - ate words we find to grieve each
Dm7
Dm7/G
G7
C
oth - er do not mean we'd leave each
F7(add6)
B♭
Gm7
Cm7
3fr
oth - er. So come fill my arms and we'll for -
rit.
a tempo

F9sus
F7
B♭6
Gm7
C9
get the mean-ing-less sor-rows each time we say we're through.
A♭9♯11
10fr
B♭maj7/F
B♭6/F
Cm7/F
8fr
Fm7
F7
B♭maj7/F
B♭6/F
Dar-ling, can't you see there can nev-er
Cm/F
3fr
Fm7
F7
B♭maj7/F
B♭6/F
Cm7
3fr
Opt.
be too man-y to-mor-rows if you
F7
N.C.
A♭6/9
G♭maj13
B♭
stay with me?
sfz

THERE'S GOTTA BE SOMETHING BETTER THAN THIS

Music by CY COLEMAN
Lyrics by DOROTHY FIELDS

A
D
C♯7
do. And when I find me some - thing
learn. And if I find me some - thing a
live. And when I find me some kind of
F♯m7
B7
A/E
C/E
bet - ter to do, I'm gon - na get up, I'm gon - na get out, I'm gon - na
half - wit can learn, I'm gon - na get up, I'm gon - na get out, I'm gon - na
life I can live, I'm gon - na get up, I'm gon - na get out, I'm gon - na
A/E
C/E
A
N.C.
To Coda
1
get up, get out and do it!
get up, get out and learn it!
get up, get out and live it!
There's got - ta be
Tambourine
2
A
Dmaj7
C♯9
F♯m7
All these jok - ers, how I hate them,

B7
C7
B7
B♭7
A7
F9
E9
HELENE:
NICKIE:
with the grop - ing, grab - bing, clutch - ing,
G♯6
A6
C7
B7
B♭7
A7
F9
E7
HELENE:
NICKIE:
HELENE:
NICKIE:
clinch - ing, stran - gling, han - dling, fum - bling,
G♯6
A6
N.C.
HELENE:
BOTH:
D.S. al Coda
pinch - ing. Phoo-ey! There's got - ta be
CODA
Em7
A
Em7
A
Em7
A

I'M THE BRAVEST INDIVIDUAL

Music by CY COLEMAN
Lyrics by DOROTHY FIELDS

Dm7
Em7
Fmaj7
Em7
Dm7
Em7
F♯m7♭5
B7
OSCAR:
I'm the brav - est in - di - vid - u - al I have ev - er met!
Em
Em(maj7)
Em7
A7
D
Dm7
CHARITY:
This game makes ver - y good sense, I get re - sults.
OSCAR:
Is - n't that great?
E♭m
E♭m(maj7)
E♭m7
A♭7
D♭
D
G7
CHARITY:
Get back my con - fi - dence and an e - ven pulse, sev - en - ty - eight.
Cmaj7
C6
B♭maj7
B♭6
So, when I pan - ic and think each day I've come to the end of the line, then

Cmaj7
Em7
A7
I say that fear has-n't licked me yet! I keep tell-ing my-self:
Dm7
Em7
Fmaj7
Em7
Dm7
G7
C
I'm the brav-est in-di-vid-u-al I have ev-er met!
Gmaj7
G6
Gmaj7
A9/G
5fr
Gmaj7
G6
Gmaj7
A9/G
5fr
Gmaj7
G6
Gmaj7
G6
Fmaj7
F6
OSCAR:
Fun-ny, but sud-den-ly I can't swal-low. I think I'm go-ing to

Fmaj7 F6 Gmaj7 G6 Gmaj7 G6
die! Some - times, if you'll par - don the word, I
Bm7(add4) E9♯11 E Am7 Bm7 Cmaj7 Bm7
6fr
CHARITY:
sweat! Then you say to your - self:
*BOTH:
I'm the brav - est in - di - vid - u - al
Am7 Bm7 Cmaj7 Bm7 Am7 Bm7
I have ev - er met!
**OSCAR:
I'm the brav - est
Cmaj7 Bm7 Am7 Bm7 C♯m7♭5 F♯7
4fr
in - di - vid - u - al I have ev - er met!
*Charity sung, Oscar spoken tentatively
**Oscar sung

Bm
Bm(maj7)
7fr
Bm7
E9
A
CHARITY:
Your game makes ver - y good sense, I get re - sults! Is - n't that fine!
Bbm
Bbm(maj7)
6fr
Bbm7/Eb
6fr
Eb7
Ab
4fr
OSCAR:
Got back my con - fi - dence and an e - ven pulse, a
D7
Gmaj7
G6
Gmaj7
G6
CHARITY:
hun - dred and nine! So when you pan - ic and feel each day you'll
Fmaj7
F6
Fmaj7
F#maj7
Gmaj7
G6
OSCAR:
fail at what - ev - er you try... I just say that

Gmaj7
G6
Bm11
E9♯11
6fr
E
CHARITY:
fear has - n't licked me yet! And keep tell - ing your - self:
Am9
5fr
Bm7
Cmaj7
Bm7
Am9
5fr
Bm7
Cmaj7
Bm7
OSCAR:
I'm the strong - est, sound - est, sto - i - cal, dar - ing - est, man - li - est, most he - ro - i - cal,
Am7
Bm7
Cmaj7
Bm7
Am7
Bm7
BOTH:
I'm the brav - est in - di - vid - u - al I have
Am7
D7
G
Am7
D7
G
ev - er met!

THE RHYTHM OF LIFE

Music by CY COLEMAN
Lyrics by DOROTHY FIELDS

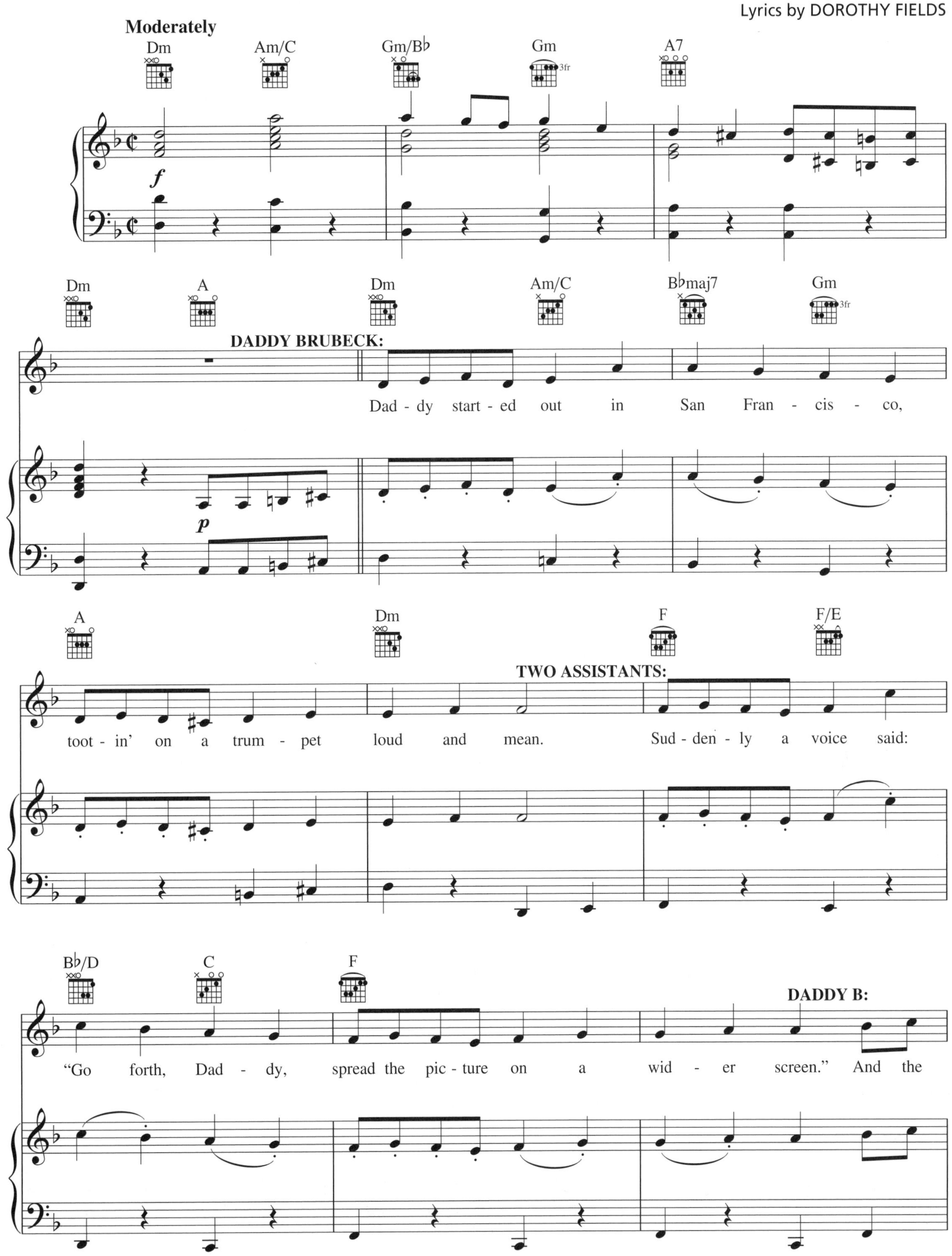

Moderately

Dm Am/C Gm/B♭ Gm A7

f

Dm A Dm Am/C B♭maj7 Gm

DADDY BRUBECK:

Dad - dy start - ed out in San Fran - cis - co,

p

A Dm F F/E

TWO ASSISTANTS:

toot - in' on a trum - pet loud and mean. Sud - den - ly a voice said:

B♭/D C F

DADDY B:

"Go forth, Dad - dy, spread the pic - ture on a wid - er screen." And the

B♭ B♭maj7/A E7/G♯ E7 Am Am7/G D7/F♯ D7
5fr
5fr
voice said: "Dad - dy, there's a mil - lion pi - geons wait - in' to be hooked on new re - li - gions.
TWO ASSISTANTS:
Dad - dy go, go, go, go.
Gm C7 Dm/A Dm Gm6/B♭ A7
3fr
Hit the road, Dad - dy, leave your com - mon law wife, spread the re - li - gion of the
Tell them ev - 'ry - thing you
Dm Fm Fm/E♭ D♭ B♭m D♭
GROUP A:
rhy - thm of life." And the rhy - thm of life is a pow - er - ful beat, puts a
know.

E♭ E♭/D♭ A♭maj7/C A♭ A♭/C D♭ D♭/C
3fr 4fr 3fr
tin - gle in your fin - gers and a tin - gle in your feet. Rhy - thm in your bed - room,
B♭m Gm7♭5 B♭m C C/E Fm
rhy - thm in the street, yes, the rhy - thm of life is a pow - er - ful beat! Oh, the
Fm E♭ D♭ B♭m D♭ E♭ D♭
3fr 3fr
rhy - thm of life is a pow - er - ful beat, puts a tin - gle in your fin - gers and a
GROUP B: To feel the rhy - thm of life, to feel the
GROUP C: Dad - dy, go, go, go,
(2nd x only)
mf

A♭maj7/C
A♭
4fr
A♭/C
3fr
D♭
D♭/C
B♭m
Gm7♭5
B♭m
tin - gle in your feet. Rhy - thm in your bed - room, rhy - thm in the street, yes, the
pow - er - ful beat, to feel the tin - gle in your fin - gers,
go. Tell them ev - 'ry -
C
C/E
1
Fm
2
Fm
rhy - thm of life is a pow - er - ful beat! Oh, the pow - er - ful beat!
to feel the tin - gle in your feet. tin - gle in your feet.
thing you know.
Dm
Am/C
B♭maj7
Gm
3fr
A
Dm
DADDY B:
Dad - dy spread the gos - pel in Mil - wau - kee, took his walk - ie talk - ie to Rock - y Ridge.
p

F
F/E
B♭/D
C
F
TWO ASSISTANTS:
Blew his way to Can - ton, then to Scran - ton, till he land - ed un - der the Man -
B♭
Gm
3fr
E7
E7/G♯
GROUP D:
hat - tan Bridge. Dad - dy was a new sen - sa - tion, got him - self a con - gre - ga - tion,
Am
Am6/G
3fr
D7/F♯
Gm
3fr
Gm7
built up quite an op - er - a - tion down be - low. With the pie - eyed pip - er blow - ing,
C7
C7/E
Dm
A7
Dm
A7
Dm
while the mus - ca - tel was flow - ing, all the cats were go - go - go - ing down be - low.

*Group E – 1st time through women only (sing top note), 2nd time add men on bottom note harmony (sung at pitch)

D
DADDY B. &
TWO ASSISTANTS:
G
Em
A7
D
Flip your wings and fly to Dad - dy! Flip your wings and fly to Dad - dy!
G
Em
A7
D
Flip your wings and fly to Dad - dy! Fly, fly, fly to Dad - dy!
D
OTHERS:
G
Em
A7
D
Take a dive and swim to Dad - dy! Take a dive and swim to Dad - dy!
mf
G
Em
A7
D
Take a dive and swim to Dad - dy! Swim, swim, swim to Dad - dy!

D
Em/G
Em
A7
D
Hit the floor and crawl to Dad - dy! Hit the floor and crawl to Dad - dy!
f
G
Em
A7
D
Hit the floor and crawl to Dad - dy! Crawl, crawl, crawl to Dad - dy!
Dm
Gm
3fr
A
Dm
Am
Am/G
F
Dm
F
GROUP A:
And the rhy - thm of life is a pow - er - ful beat, puts a
mp

G
G/F
Cmaj7/E
C
C/E
F
F/E
tin - gle in your fin - gers and a tin - gle in your feet. Rhy - thm in your bed - room,
Dm
Bm7♭5
Dm
E
E/G♯
Am
rhy - thm in the street, yes, the rhy - thm of life is a pow - er - ful beat! And the
Am/G
F
Dm
F
G
G/F
rhy - thm of life is a pow - er - ful beat, puts a tin - gle in your fin - gers and a
GROUP B:
To feel the rhy - thm of life, to feel the
GROUP C: (2nd x only)
Dad - dy go, go, go,
mf

Cmaj7/E
C
C/E
F
F/E
Dm
Bm7♭5
Dm
tin - gle in your feet. Rhy - thm in your bed - room, rhy - thm in the street, yes, the
pow - er - ful beat, to feel the tin - gle in your fin - gers,
go. Tell them ev - 'ry -
E
E/G♯
1
Am
2
Am
A7
rhy - thm of life is a pow - er - ful beat! And the pow - er - ful beat!
to feel the tin - gle in your feet. tin - gle in your feet.
thing you know.
Dm
Gm
3fr
C7
F
B:
A:
C:
ALL:
To feel the rhy - thm of life, to feel the pow - er - ful beat,
f

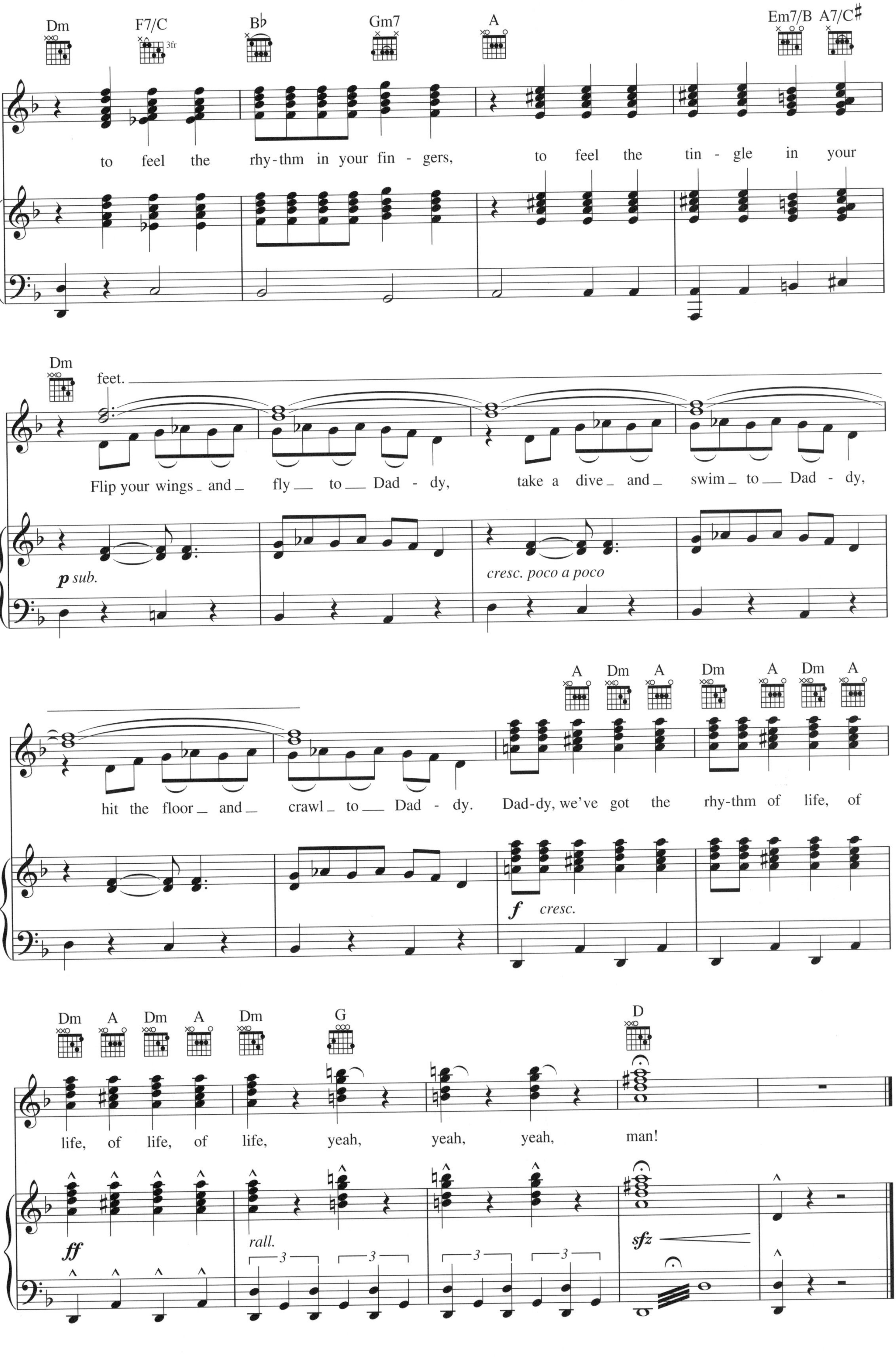

Dm F7/C B♭ Gm7 A Em7/B A7/C♯

to feel the rhy-thm in your fin - gers, to feel the tin - gle in your

Dm

feet.

Flip your wings and fly to Dad - dy, take a dive and swim to Dad - dy,

p sub. *cresc. poco a poco*

hit the floor and crawl to Dad - dy.

A Dm A Dm A Dm A

Dad-dy, we've got the rhy-thm of life, of

f *cresc.*

Dm A Dm A Dm G D

life, of life, of life, yeah, yeah, yeah, man!

ff *rall.* *sfz*

A GOOD IMPRESSION

Music by CY COLEMAN
Lyrics by DOROTHY FIELDS

Lightly jaunty
F
Em7♭5
A7sus
A7
Dm7
G7
Gm7
Am7
B♭maj7
Bm7
You might say to your-self, "This man is dif-f'rent, this ap-proach is new."
mf
Cm7
3fr
B♭maj7
E♭9
So, I'm will-ing to make a small con-fes-sion: I'm de-ter-mined to make a
C7
good im-pres-sion on you.
(whistling)
D7
D7/F♯
C9sus/G
N.C.
straight 8ths

BABY DREAM YOUR DREAM

Music by CY COLEMAN
Lyrics by DOROTHY FIELDS

C
C+
NICKIE: Dream we sign the lease, leave a small de - pos - it.
BOTH: Three fat hun - gry kids, all in pink con - di - tion.
Am
C7
HELENE: Three and one - half rooms with a walk - in clos - et.
HELENE: So! who's in the "red?" NICKIE: That nice ob - ste - tri - cian.
F
C/E
Bm7♭5
E7
BOTH:
We'll ask the lo - cal jet set to dine on our di - nette set.
Big Dad - dy's fa - v'rite pas - time, he's had it for the last time.
Am
Am(maj7)/E
Am7
D7
Gm
Gm(maj7)/D
Gm7
C7
NICKIE: Right a - cross the street there's a friend - ly bank, you
BOTH: Soon Dad - dy don't come home. He says he's gone bowl - ing,

F Fmaj7/C F6 Dm7b5 G7
make a friend - ly loan, HELENE: and the bank says, "Thank you."
but a bowl - ing ball NICKIE: is not what Dad - dy's roll - ing.
C C+
BOTH:
Ev - 'ry Sat - ur - day we'll spend all our mon - ey.
Ev - 'ry night they fight. Once they both ex - plod - ed,
Am C7
HELENE: Join the P. T. A. NICKIE: They will love you, hon - ey.
then they both got tight. HELENE: Tight? Hell, they got load - ed.
F E7/B E7 Am Am7/D D7
BOTH:
Life will be fro - zen peach - es and cream, ba - by,
Well, who knows what will sour the cream when you

1
Dm7
G13
3fr
C6/9
Cmaj7/B
5fr
Am7
C6/G
dream
your
dream.
2
Dm7
G13
3fr
C9
C13♯11
3fr
dream
your...
But come to
rit.
Freely, straight eighths
F6
B♭9♯11
Em7
C/E
think of it, how hap - py I would be if some-day I could find the kind of guy who'd
A7
A♭7(add13)
4fr
Slow 4, somewhat freely
D♭
say to me: Ba - by, dream your dream,
rit.

D♭+
B♭m/D♭
HELENE:
close your eyes and try it. Dream of three fat kids.
D♭7
NICKIE:
Broth - er, would I buy it!
Slower, freely
G♭maj7
G♭7
F7sus
F7
BOTH:
Life could be fro - zen peach - es and
B♭m
E♭
cream,
NICKIE:
if on - ly I could,
HELENE:
if on - ly I could...
E♭m7/A♭
BOTH:
dream, dream, dream a dream.
D♭
D♭6/9

SWEET CHARITY

G
C9
Bm7
G
F♯7♭9(no3rd)
3fr
hav - ing you a - round,
Sweet Char - i - ty!
Bm7
Bm(maj7)
7fr
Bm7
Bm7♭5
E7♯5(♭9)
6fr
Warm words I've nev - er said
late - ly
Am7
F9
E9
pop off the top of my head.
In - cred - i - ble!
Am7
D7♯5(♭9)
4fr
Am7
D7
If, by and by, you and I should be we,

G6/9
Bm
E9♯5
E9
E7
I could touch the sky quite eas - i - ly.
A13
D7♯9
D9
B7♭13
E7♭9
E7
So, if you are free, Sweet Char - i - ty,
A13
D7♯9
D9
B7
E7
please be - long to me, sweet, Sweet Char - i - ty,
rall.
Slower
A13
D13
G
C9
Gmaj9
please be - long to me.

WHERE AM I GOING

Music by CY COLEMAN
Lyrics by DOROTHY FIELDS

F♯m7
B7
Emaj7
C9
Gm7
C7
Ain't it a shame? But no one's to blame but my - self!
Which way is clear when you've
Eb9
Bbm7
lost your way year af - ter year?
Do I keep fall - ing in love for just the kick of it,

E♭9
B♭m7
Am7
D7
stag - ger - ing through
the thin and thick of it,
hat - ing each old and
Am7
D7
Am7
D7
tir - ed trick of it?
Know what I am?
I'm good and sick of it!
G
G/F♯
Em7
G/D
Where am I go - ing?
Why do I care?
mf
C♯m7♭5
Em/F♯
F♯7
Bm7
B♭7
Run to the Bronx or Wash - ing - ton Square,
no mat - ter where I run,

Am7
D7
Dm7/G
I meet my - self there, look - ing in - side me.
A7/C♯
Adim/C
G/B
What do I see?
An - ger and hope and doubt.
Em
Am7
Am/D
What am I all a - bout and where am I go - ing?
You tell
G5
Am7/G
G(add2)
Am7/G
Gm7
Cmaj7/G
G5
me!
cresc.
dim.
p

I'M A BRASS BAND

Music by CY COLEMAN
Lyrics by DOROTHY FIELDS

Moderately slow
Moderately bright, not fast
C7
Db7/Ab
Gm
F
Db7/Ab
last. Now I'm a brass band, I'm a harp - si - chord,
mp
poco accel.
Gm
C7
Fm7
Bb7
I'm a clar - i - net!
Em7
A7
Ebm7
Ab7
I'm the Phil - a - del - phia Or - ches - tra,
Dm7
G7
Gm7/C
C7
Db7
I'm the Mod - ern Jazz Quar - tet.

Gm
3fr
C7
F
I'm the band from Ma - cy's big pa - rade, a
Em7
A7
D7
wild Count Bas - ie blast.
I'm the
Gm7
A♭dim7
3
bells of Saint Pe - ter's in Rome,
I'm
F/A
A7
Dm
Dm/C
D7/C
tis - sue pa - per on a comb,
and

B♭6
B♭dim7
3
all kinds of mu - sic keeps
F/A
A+
Dm
G7
pour - ing out of me 'cause
Gm11/C
3fr
some - bod - y loves me at
F
Gm
3fr
Fm/A♭
B♭
C7
F6
last.
cresc.
f

I LOVE TO CRY AT WEDDINGS

Music by CY COLEMAN
Lyrics by DOROTHY FIELDS

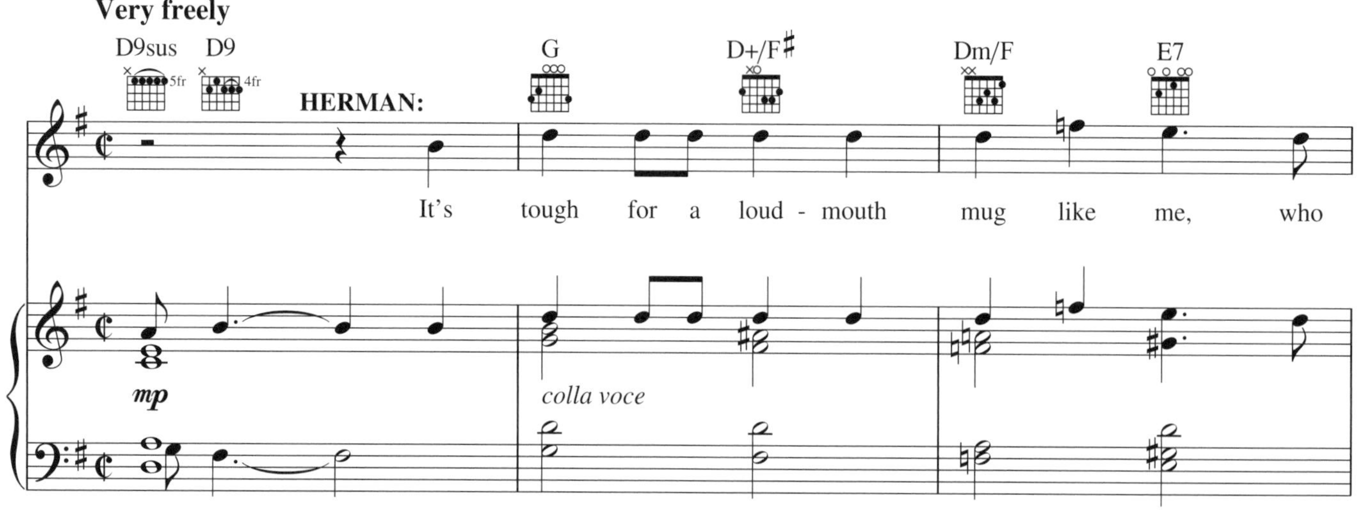

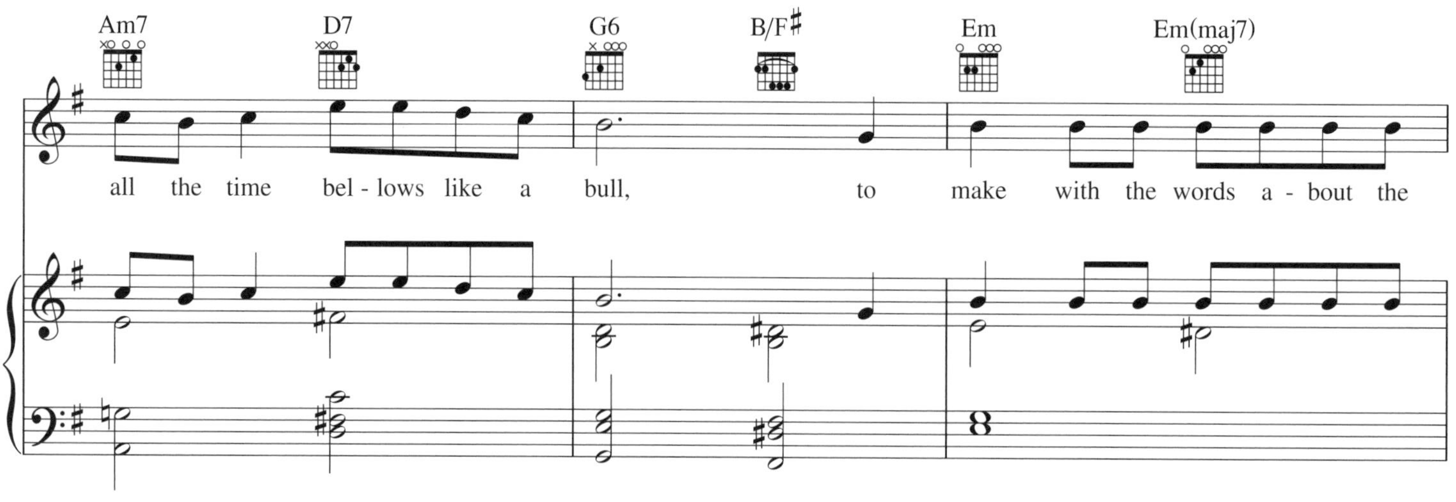

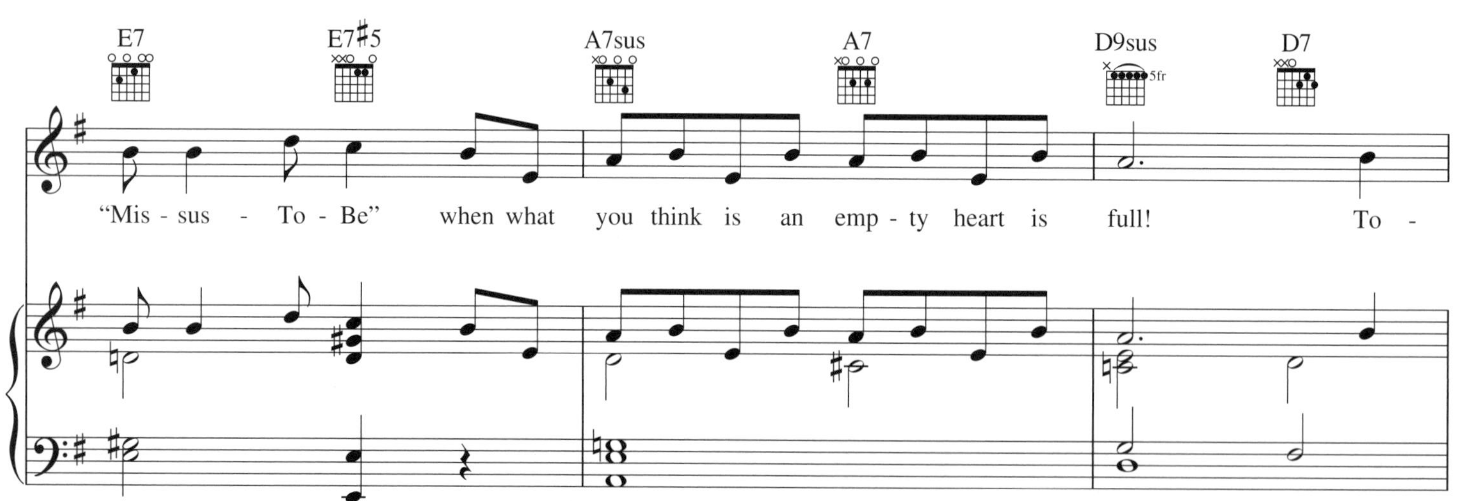

Am7
D13
A7(add13)
(falsetto)
mor - row when you say, "I do," I'll die! I'm al - most too a - shamed to tell you
D9
B♭dim7
Moderately bright 2
D7
G
why! I love to cry at wed - dings, how I love to cry at
mf
Gdim/B♭
D7
G
wed - dings. I walk in - to a chap - el and get hap - pi - ly hys -
Gdim/B♭
D7
TENOR SOLO:
HERMAN:
ter - i - cal. The ush - ers and at - ten - dants, the

G6
F#7
HERMAN:
fam - i - ly de - pen - dents, I see them and I start to sniff. Have
Bm
Dm7
G7
TENOR SOLO:
HERMAN:
you an ex - tra hand - ker - chief? And all through the ser - vice, while the
Cmaj7
C6
Bm7
E7
HERMAN:
bride and groom look ner - vous, tears of joy are stream - ing down my
A7
E♭
3fr
D7
B7
Em
Em(maj7)
TENOR SOLO:
HERMAN:
face. I love to cry at wed - dings,
Down his face.

Em7
A7
Am7
Am7/D
D7
an - y - bod - y's wed - ding, an - y - time, an - y - where, an - y
G
C♯dim7
F7
ROSIE:
place! I al - ways weep at wed - dings, I'm a
B♭
F7
sog - gy creep at wed - dings. Ah, what's as sweet and slop - py as, "oh,
B♭6
F7
TWO HOSTESSES:
prom - ise me," and all that jazz? The man you rest your head with, the

B♭(add2)
3fr
A7
man you share your bed with is mar - ried to you, so you know he
Dm
Fm7
B♭9
NICKIE:
HELENE:
won't jump up and dress and blow! I could mar - ry Her - man... and be
E♭maj7
3fr
E♭6
Dm7
NICKIE:
per - ma - nent - ly sor - ry. We would make a
G7
N.C.
G♭7
F7
D
real - ly lous - y pair. But,

Gm
Gm(maj7)
Gm7
C7
ALL:
gee, I want a wed - ding, an - y kind of wed - ding, an - y -
Cm7
Cm7/F
B♭6/9
time, an - y place, an - y - where!
And
B♭m7
E♭7
A♭maj7
A♭6
all through the ser - vice, while the bride and groom look ner - vous,
Gm7
C7
F7
G7
G7♭5
tears of joy are stream - ing down my face.
I

Cm
3fr
Cm(maj7)
8fr
Cm7
3fr
love to cry at wed - dings, an - y - bod - y's
Cm6
3fr
Fm7
wed - ding, an - y - time,
an - y -
cresc.
A♭/B♭
4fr
E♭
3fr
where,
an - y place!
f
E♭6
A♭/B♭
4fr
E♭6
E♭
3fr